HAL•LEONARD® VIOLIN PLAY-ALONG

AUDIO ACCESS INCLUDED

PLAYBACK+
Speed • Pitch • Balance • Loop

UPDATED EDITION **VOL. 37**

TAYLOR SWIFT

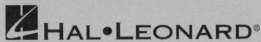

To access online content visit:
www.halleonard.com/mylibrary

Enter Code
6036-7088-9992-4011

ISBN 978-1-4803-2440-4

HAL•LEONARD®

7777 W. BLUEMOUND RD. P.O. BOX 13819 MILWAUKEE, WI 53213

In Australia Contact:
Hal Leonard Australia Pty. Ltd.
4 Lentara Court
Cheltenham, Victoria, 3192 Australia
 Email: ausadmin@halleonard.com.au

Visit Hal Leonard Online at
www.halleonard.com

Photography by Brian Doben © 2012
Firefly Entertainment, Inc.
All Rights Reserved

Jon Vriesacker, violin
Audio Arrangements by Peter Deneff
Produced and Recorded by
Jake Johnson at Paradyme Productions

Hal•Leonard®

VIOLIN
PLAY-ALONG

AUDIO
ACCESS
INCLUDED

UPDATED EDITION

VOL. 37

TAYLOR SWIFT

CONTENTS

Blank Space

Words and Music by Taylor Swift, Max Martin and Shellback

I Knew You Were Trouble

Words and Music by Taylor Swift, Shellback and Max Martin

Mean

Words and Music by Taylor Swift

We Are Never Ever Getting Back Together

Words and Music by Taylor Swift, Shellback and Max Martin

Our Song

Words and Music by Taylor Swift

White Horse

Words and Music by Taylor Swift and Liz Rose

You Belong With Me

Words and Music by Taylor Swift and Liz Rose

Shake It Off
Words and Music by Taylor Swift, Max Martin and Shellback